ECOLOGY ALERT!

Farming

Jane Featherstone

RAINTREE
STECK-VAUGHN
PUBLISHERS
A Steck-Vaughn Company

Austin, Texas

Ecology Alert!

Coasts	Farming
Communities	Transportation
Energy	Rivers

Cover: Spraying pesticide on lemon trees

Title page: Using a combine harvester to harvest a crop of oats

Contents page: Shearing a sheep

Published by Raintree Steck-Vaughn Publishers, an imprint of Steck-Vaughn Company

Library of Congress Cataloging-in-Publication Data
Featherstone, Jane.
Farming / Jane Featherstone.
    p.   cm.—(Ecology Alert)
Includes bibliographical references and index.
Summary: Discusses various kinds of farming, including livestock farming and sustainable farming, and examines the changing nature of how the land is used and preserved. Includes case studies and activities.
ISBN 0-8172-5371-8
1. Agriculture—Juvenile literature.
2. Agriculture—Environmental aspects—Juvenile literature.
[1. Farms. 2. Farm life. 3. Agriculture]
I. Title. II. Series.
S519.F435   2000
630—dc21   98-25837

Printed in Italy. Bound in the United States.
1 2 3 4 5 6 7 8 9 0 03 02 01 00 99

Picture acknowledgments
Birdlife International (Mark Edwards) 10; Chapel Studios (Zul Mukhida) 23; Ecoscene (David Wootton) 7; Eye Ubiquitous (Chloe Johnson) 5 top, (Skjold) 9, (D. Gill) 15, (Jill Hazel) 28; Getty Images (Zane Williams) 1, (Jon Gray) 4, (Andy Sacks) 6, (Gary John Norman) 10, (David Hiser) 14, (Gary Irving) 18, (David Joel) 22, (Siegried Eigstler) 25, (Brian Atkinson) 26; Impact Photos (Jorn Stjerneklar) 8, (Jorn Stjerneklar) 11, (Christine Bluntzer) 12, (Rhonda Klevansky) 13, (David Reed) 19, (Mike McQueen) 20, (Rachel Morton) 27; Margot Richardson 21 (both); Wayland Picture Library 3, 5 (bottom), 24. Artwork by Peter Bull Art Studio.

Contents

Food for Thought

How does your family choose what food to buy? Do you ever think about where your food has come from? Do you ask yourself "How was it grown?" or "Who grew it?" Do you know if growing it did any damage to the environment?

Nowadays, stores and supermarkets offer a huge variety of foods from all over the world. But how we choose our food could have important effects on the environment, people's health, and animal welfare. To be able to make choices, you need to have information so that you can make up your mind. This book is a start. In it you will find information about food, farming, and the environment.

The food we buy in stores has been grown by farmers all over the world.

Let's go back to that supermarket shelf. It is very difficult sometimes to see the connection between slices of meat and an animal, or a loaf of bread and the soil, or a bottle of milk and a cow.

How does food get to supermarkets, and why does it look the way it does? It is important to know what happens to the food you eat and what happens to the environment where it was farmed.

How it all began

The agricultural revolution took place about 10,000 years ago. Before then, people were just like other animals. They found and ate the food that nature provided by killing wild animals and gathering fruit, vegetables, and seeds from wherever they happened to grow. This took a lot of effort. Everybody was involved in finding food. Not many people could live in one area because food was scarce.

Then, people discovered that if they planted seeds in the soil, they could wait for the seeds to grow and harvest the crop, such as wheat. Growing plants and keeping animals allowed people to become farmers and live in one place. Gradually, farmers learned how to grow more and more food on the same amount of land.

▲ Harvesting a crop of rice in Nepal

▼ Keeping animals means that people can control their food supply.

Getting better at farming

After the Industrial Revolution, which began about 1780, farmers in wealthier countries began using machines such as tractors and combine harvesters. Machines meant that more work could be done by less people.

Farmers also learned to use chemicals. Fertilizers make soil more fertile so that more crops can be grown. Pesticides kill harmful insects that eat plants or cause diseases. Herbicides get rid of weeds that grow in the wrong place.

In wealthy countries such as the United States and Great Britain, farmers now produce much more food from the land than in the past. Today, a small number of people can produce enough food for a large population. This means that most people can do other work. They can live together in towns and cities. Civilizations still depend on farming to feed people in towns, who do not grow their own food.

An aerial photograph of combine harvesters in a wheat field, harvesting a crop of wheat

What is the problem?

Despite the way farming has developed, it is often difficult for farmers to make a living. In some countries, land and farming supplies are expensive, but prices paid for food are low. In other countries, there is not enough good-quality farmland to feed the people.

On the other hand, people are worried about the environment. For example, soil is being lost or damaged. Pesticides kill many insects and animals. Herbicides kill all sorts of plants, not just weeds. Many chemicals remain in the food we eat.

People are beginning to want more than cheap food from farmers. We want farmers to protect the environment and to treat animals well. Many farmers also want to do this, but it is already difficult for them to make a living. Perhaps if we all think a bit more about how our food is grown, things can be worked out in a way that is better for everyone.

Many animals, such as pigs, are farmed intensively. This means they are kept in small pens, where they cannot move around.

Feeding the World

The food we eat every day makes up our diet. A balanced diet is one that keeps us healthy. It is made up of carbohydrates, fats, proteins, vitamins, minerals, water, and fiber. No single type of food has all these nutrients. So we need to balance our diet by eating different kinds of foods.

Enough food for everyone

The world has a population of about 5.5 billion people. More than 2 billion people do not have the correct kinds of food to keep them healthy. More than 500 million people cannot get enough food of any kind.

When crops fail to grow or countries are at war, people can die of hunger. These people in Somalia are waiting for food to be given to them.

However, there is actually enough food in the world to feed everyone. The real problem with hunger is how food is shared among people and how much it costs. People with enough money can always get enough to eat.

Calories Around the World

Calories measure the amount of energy in food. The average person needs to eat about 2,350 calories per day to stay healthy.

● In the United States, the average person eats about 3,650 calories per day.

● In Bangladesh, the average person eats about 1,925 calories per day.

Activity

You are what you eat

What do you eat? Make a list of everything you eat in one day. Copy the headings below. Put a check in each column to show which nutrients are in each food. You will find what food contains by looking at the label on the packages or in science books.

FOOD/DRINK   Protein   Carbohydrate   Minerals   Vitamins

Are you eating a balanced diet? Of the food you ate, which came from plants and which came from animals?

Although we can get all the food we need from plants, people around the world also like to eat meat.

Cereals: the food for life

Cereals are grains such as wheat, rice, and corn. They are the most important food for most of the world. Cereals are a good source of energy, protein, minerals, and vitamins. They make a good basic diet.

What about meat?

Meat is also rich in body-building protein and vitamins. People in wealthier countries can afford to eat meat. The way to produce a lot of meat is to farm animals intensively. If farm animals and chickens are kept in pens and fed grain, such as wheat and oats, it will make them grow more quickly or lay more eggs.

Feeding grain to animals

About 40 percent of the grain grown in the world is fed to animals. This is a problem because the poor of the world cannot afford to buy meat. In Mexico, for example, one person out of every five people has a very poor diet. The cereals Mexicans could afford are being fed to animals.

Good farming keeps animals on land that cannot be used to grow crops or uses animals to graze land as part of crop rotation. This is because animals can digest grass, which humans cannot. Animals turn the grass into food such as milk and meat. People can then eat this protein-rich food.

But is it good farming to grow cereal crops on good land and then feed them to animals instead of to people?

Intensively farmed chickens eating grain

Eating Cereals
The average Chinese family gets nearly three quarters of its calories from cereals.
The average American family gets less than one quarter of its calories from cereals.

Cattle Farming in Namibia

Every country needs to feed its people. But in some countries, this is difficult because the natural environment limits what can be grown.

Namibia, in southern Africa, is a very dry country. It does not have any rivers except on its borders. There is very little rain, and high temperatures mean that the soil dries out quickly. The soil is poor. Only coarse grass, bushes, and trees grow.

It is too dry to grow large areas of crops. One of the few things that can be farmed are cattle, for meat. There are only 1.4 million people living in Namibia, but there are 2 million cattle. Each cow needs about 17 gal. (45 l) of water a day. Most of the water comes from under the ground, in wells.

Mr. Agenbach owns a large commercial cattle farm near Tsumeb. It covers 12,350 acres (5,000 ha). The land is so poor that one cow needs 37 acres (15 ha) to find enough to eat. Mr. Agenbach sells all his cattle for profit and buys in all his food.

Mr. Indongo has a small farm near Oshakati. He grows just enough food to feed his family. He has two cows and three goats, but it is hard for his animals to find enough to eat, so they do not give much milk or manure to fertilize the plants.

Growing enough to make a living is hard for both farmers, but on Namibia's difficult land there are not many alternatives.

Cattle in Namibia. Cattle farming is one of the few ways of using the land.

Using the Land, Losing the Soil

Do you ever think about the ground beneath your feet? Nearly everything you eat comes from the soil. Plants need soil to grow. Animals need plants to eat.

What is soil?

Soil is made when rocks are broken down into sand, silt, and clay. Rotting plants and animals add organic material. Microscopic creatures in the soil change the organic material into nutrients that the plants can use. This is the soil cycle. All living things end up in the soil. It is a living material.

New soil is being made all the time. But it is a very slow process. It takes from 3,000 to 12,000 years to make a layer of soil that can be used by farmers. Yet soil is being lost all the time through erosion.

A farmer in China plows the soil using donkeys.

Soil erosion

Today, farming is the cause of most soil erosion. This is because plants and trees that hold the soil together are cleared to grow crops. Sometimes, the soil is left bare, and, when it rains or is windy, the soil is easily whisked away.

The main reasons plants and trees are cleared are because of deforestation and overgrazing.

Overgrazing

Overgrazing happens when animals eat all the grass and plants and leave the soil bare. This occurs in some places because too many animals are grazing on the same plot of land.

Soil erosion in Malawi. The soil has been washed away by the rain.

Settlers in Guatemala clear rain forest to use the land for farming. They are using a method called slash and burn.

Deforestation

A lot of soil is lost when forests are cleared from the land. In some countries this happened a long time ago when land was cleared for farms, towns, and cities. Today, it is happening in many developing countries. Sometimes the trees are cut down so the lumber can be sold. Sometimes the trees are cleared by farmers.

Deforestation in tropical countries is leading to huge soil loss. The soils are often thin and lie on steep slopes. The heavy tropical rains wash away the soil, often causing mud slides and flooding.

Land Loss

In the world, every year

- 25 million acres (10 million ha) of forest trees are being lost, which exposes the soil to erosion;
- Rain and wind carry away 23 billion tons of soil.

Soil loss caused by farming

Soil is also being lost because of the way farmers till or plow the soil. Deep plowing loosens the soil to a great depth, making it easier for it to be eroded.

The structure of the soil is also being changed through intensive methods of farming. Heavy machinery flattens the soil and squeezes out the air and water. Some pesticides kill the microscopic creatures that live in the soil. Chemical fertilizers are being used instead of organic fertilizers, such as manure, on the soil.

Huge machines such as these combine harvesters can damage soil because they are so heavy.

Managing the Kilum Mountain Forest

The Kilum Mountain Forest is in the northwest of Cameroon, West Africa. The climate is cool and pleasant, and the soil is very fertile. Most of the people are subsistence farmers. They grow many crops, including rice, corn, and cocoyams.

However, the population is growing, so more of the forest is being cleared for farming. This farmland is suffering from soil erosion. Many local people have become worried about the loss of the forest and of the soil. They started the Kilum Mountain Forestry Project to take care of the land.

People using an A-frame in Kilum Mountain Forest, Cameroon. A stone hangs on a piece of string from the top of the frame. When the frame is on level ground, the stone hangs in the middle of the crossbar.

Part of the project is to make flat terraces of soil around the hillside. Since the terraces are level, rather than on a slope, they will keep the soil from being washed away by rain. To check that the terraces are level, the people use a simple wooden frame, in the shape of an "A," with a crossbar in the middle. There is a photograph of an A-frame above.

Conserving soil

Soil is a valuable resource. Farming and the production of food depend upon soil. It is important that we treat soil with respect and that we conserve soils and make the best possible use of them.

Activity

Testing soil erosion

Find four cardboard boxes. They should be about 20 in. (50 cm) long, 12 in. (30 cm) wide and 4 in. (10 cm) deep. Line them with foil to make them waterproof. At one end of each box cut a V shape about 1.5 in. (3.5 cm) deep. Fill three boxes with soil.

Box 1: Smooth the surface of the soil.
Box 2: Make furrows parallel to the short sides of the box.
Box 3: Make furrows that run the length of the box.
Box 4: Fill with some grass growing in soil taken from a lawn or field.

Make each box a slope by lifting it about 2 in. (5 cm) at one end. Place a bowl under the V-shaped end.

Use a watering can to sprinkle water gently at the top end of each box. Compare how much soil is carried down into the bowl.

Box 1

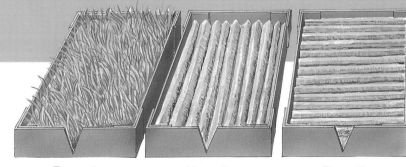

Box 4   Box 3   Box 2

Arable and Livestock Farming

Arable farming is growing food crops. The main food crops are grains and cereals, roots and tubers (such as potatoes), vegetables, fruits, and beans. Others are tea, coffee, and sugar. Farmers also grow crops to provide materials we need, such as cotton for cloth or trees for lumber.

Livestock farming is the rearing of animals, birds, or game. They give us meat, eggs, and milk. They are also raised for wool and other products.

This farm in Illinois is an arable and a livestock farm. You can see crops and a barn for animals.

Activity

Farm visit

Plan a visit to a local farm. Try to get a map of the farm before you visit. Put on the map how each field is used. Is it used for growing crops or for grazing animals? Does this change from year to year? Is there a pattern?

Find out how each building is used. Is the barn used for storing crops or for keeping cattle inside in the winter?

Plan some questions you would like to ask the farmer. These might include

- How many animals do you keep?
- How do you take care of them?
- What crops do you grow?
- Do you use a fertilizer on the land?
- Do you do any conservation work on your farm?

Growing crops today

New varieties of cereal plants that give bigger crops have been developed by scientists. Large quantities of grains and other arable crops, such as potatoes and vegetables, are grown on huge fields of a single crop. This is called intensive farming.

Artificial fertilizers are put on the soil to feed the plants, and other chemicals are used to kill insects and diseases. All these chemicals can be dangerous to the health of animals and humans if not used correctly. By not putting organic material back into the soil, the nature of the soil is changed and it can be eroded more easily. Rain can wash chemicals from the soil into rivers. This pollutes the water.

Farmworkers wearing protective masks and clothing spray chemicals onto coffee plants.

Modern Farming Facts

7.5 billion acres (3 billion ha) of land are used for grazing animals.

3.7 billion acres (1.5 billion ha) of land are used for growing crops.

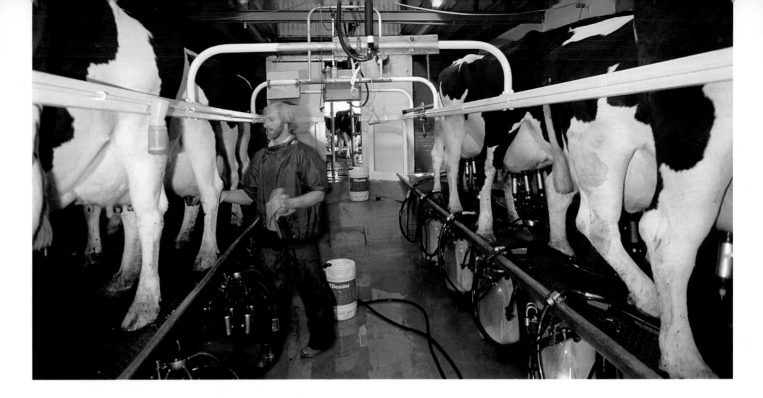

Dairy cows are bred to produce as much milk as possible. Machines are often used for milking so that many cows can be kept on one farm.

Farming livestock

Most people think of farm animals living happily in green fields or in a farmyard. This is not always what happens. Many animals are kept indoors in small pens. They often cannot move, forage for food, lie down, or meet other animals.

These are not wild animals. They have been bred by farmers. Because of intensive farming methods, their bodies have been forced to do much more than they would do if left to nature.

A dairy cow produces ten times as much milk. Chickens lay about 300 eggs a year, five to ten times more than they would do naturally. Pigs and chickens fed on grain grow quickly, so they provide cheap meat. Many people think that this method of farming does not show respect to animals.

Effects of intensive farming

Keeping animals close together gives disease a chance to spread. Farmers give their animals antibiotics and other medicines to keep them healthy. People are worried that these medicines will be passed on to humans in meat and other products.

Keeping animals indoors and in a small space produces large amounts of animal waste, called slurry. Slurry does not go into the sewage system like human waste. Slurry can be a good fertilizer, but a farm may not be able to use all that the animals make. Some slurry gets washed into rivers, causing water pollution.

A single cow can produce 10 tons of manure each year.

CASE STUDY

Chicken farm

Michael Vine runs a mixed farm in Sussex, England. He keeps cattle, sheep, and horses, but the main activity is rearing chickens for meat. At any one time he keeps 1,000 to 2,000 birds, which is a small number for a commercial chicken farm.

▲ One-day-old chicks

Mr. Vine buys chicks when they are one day old. They are kept in sheds that measure about 16 x 20 ft. (5 x 6 m), and which let in natural daylight. The chickens can move about on the floor, which is covered in wood shavings. They eat a low-protein mix that is bought in from a feed supplier. A medicine to fight bronchitis can be added to their drinking water.

▼ Chickens farmed for their meat grow very quickly. The birds below are four weeks old.

The chickens are grown until they are at least six weeks old, when they weigh about 3.5 lbs (1.6 kg), or up until they are 15 weeks old, when they weigh about 11 lbs. (5 kg). Then they are killed on the farm, and sold to local people, butcher's shops, and restaurants.

Mr. Vine has tried free-range farming, letting the chickens live outdoors for some of the time. However, it didn't work very well. "The extra fences add a lot to the cost," he says. "People aren't willing to pay more for the chickens. They want food to be as cheap as possible."

Changing Nature

A new revolution in farming is taking place. Scientists have worked out how to alter the very nature of plants and animals.

Genes are contained in every cell of all living things. They control all the information about a plant, animal, or person, from their possible height and color, to whether they are likely to catch certain diseases.

Now scientists can work out the pattern of genes in a plant or animal. For example, they can work out which gene makes a tomato red. Even more amazingly, they can move genes around within plants and animals. In theory, they could make a blue tomato or a pink sheep.

This is called genetic engineering and is a form of a new type of science, called biotechnology.

A scientist working on plants in a greenhouse

However, many people are worried about experimenting with genes in this way because it seems as though scientists are interfering with nature. Other people are worried that the new plants could breed with wild plants and create even more plants that might not be safe.

What do scientists think?
Scientists say they do research because they are curious about the world. Some scientists say that it is not up to them to think about the consequences of their work.

What do you think?
Maybe all genetically engineered food should have a clear label so that people can choose whether to buy it. For example, in Europe, a branch of the European Union has decided that it would be a good idea to label all foods that contain genetically engineered material.

Monsanto

Monsanto is a business based in St. Louis, Missouri. In 1996 it employed 28,000 people in 100 countries.

Monsanto has spent a great deal of money on scientific research into biotechnology for farming. One of its products is Roundup, a herbicide that kills weeds.

Monsanto has also developed plants such as New Leaf potatoes and Yeildgard corn that can resist attacks by insects better than other types of potatoes or corn. It has also developed Roundup Ready soya beans that are designed to be resistant to Roundup herbicide. This means that the poison kills the weeds, but does not harm the soya-bean plants. These soya beans are being used in many different types of factory-made food, all over the world.

The company says it is helping to solve the world's food and environmental problems. It believes that feeding the world in the future is only possible with biotechnology and chemistry.

Some scientists believe that the only way to feed the world is to use biotechnology to increase food production.

Biotechnology and biodiversity

Biodiversity is the variety of plants and animals in the natural world. It is important to keep biodiversity: that is, not to lose any plant or animal species.

Scientists cannot create genes. They can only use the genes that have developed naturally in plants and animals. In the past, 5,000 food plants used to be grown worldwide. Now, twenty of them provide most of the world's diet. Biotechnology will probably reduce biodiversity even more because farmers will all grow the same few plants.

There has been a huge variety of plant and animal species for thousands of years. If they die out, the species cannot be replaced.

Activity

Biodiversity in the school

Has your school an area of grass, a garden, or a playing field? Or is there a park nearby? This is an activity to find out how many different varieties of grass and other plants grow there.

1   Make a square frame out of cardboard or wood. It should be about 3 ft. (1 m) square.
2   Place the frame on an area of ground with grass and plants growing. Count every different plant you find. You do not need to know the names of the plants.
3   Now choose another piece of land that is managed in a different way from the one you have already used. Count the plants in the same way.
4   Compare your two counts. What did you find? Is there a difference in the number of plants? Why do you think this is? What could be done to encourage biodiversity?

Sustainable Farming

People all over the world are becoming more aware about the harm being done to the environment by things people do, such as farming. Methods of farming need to change so that they do not cause damage. This new way of thinking is now known as sustainable farming.

There are a growing number of people who want to buy food that has not been sprayed with chemicals or grown in factory farms. As a result, there are a growing number of farmers who are trying out methods of sustainable farming.

Organic farming

People who farm organically aim to take care of the environment. They do not use artificial pesticides and fertilizers. They avoid any pollution, pay attention to animal welfare, and look after wildlife habitats and the natural parts of their farm.

Organic farms are found in countries all over the world, from Egypt to the United States. These farmers work using strict regulations and produce many different organic foods, including fruit, vegetables, meat, milk, beans, and grains.

Organic food is usually more expensive than food produced by intensive farming. Some people are willing to pay extra for food that they feel is healthier.

Organic farming

The Be Wise Ranch is a family farm near San Diego, California. It has been run since 1977 by Bill Brammer, who grows about sixty different types of fruits and vegetables, from cabbages to avocados and melons to strawberries.

Bill says: "Our fields are fertilized with compost and rock minerals. We also use leaf sprays of kelp, fish and plant extracts, calcium, and other minerals.

"We have found that if the soil and plants get balanced nutrients, we have fewer pest problems. We believe that because of our soil quality, our produce is more nutritious, has better flavor, and lasts longer than nonorganic produce."

About three quarters of the fruits and vegetables are sold to shops or supermarkets. The rest go directly to local people under a program called Community Supported Agriculture. About 900 different families buy "shares" in the farm's harvest. The shares are packed in boxes at the farm once a week. The boxes are then delivered to various pick-up points in nearby towns and cities. Unlike supermarket food, everything in the box is grown in season at the farm.

This way, local people can enjoy fresh food, while supporting the use of environmentally friendly farming methods.

Organic farmers use natural ways to keep soil fertile. This farmer is spreading manure on his vegetable field.

Mixed farming combines crops and livestock. The fields get a rest from growing crops. The animals live outdoors, and their manure fertilizes the soil.

Mixed farming

Many farmers, both organic and nonorganic, are experimenting with mixed farming. This is a return to older methods, where animals and crops are grown on the same farm. Some fields are sown with grass to give the soil a rest from producing crops. Animals graze on the grass. Different crops are grown each year. This reduces pests and weeds. Manure from the animals is used as a fertilizer.

Antierosion plowing

We have already read about ways to reduce soil erosion on hills, by plowing around slopes rather than up and down them. Another method of plowing, called conservation tillage, is being developed. This means that the soil is not plowed as deeply. This keeps it from being lost as easily.

Asking for change

If farming is to change, it will be because consumers—that is, the people who buy food—ask for changes.

We can all choose what we buy. Our choices put pressure on store owners and farmers. For example, if everyone refused to buy meat or eggs grown on factory farms, farmers and stores would not be able to sell them at all. They would have to stop producing them in that way.

Today, farmers can use the best of both modern and older farming methods for the benefit of the environment, animal welfare, and people's health. By choosing what to buy, and what not to buy, we can all help make sure that our food is produced in ways that we find acceptable.

Activity

Make a compost column

Compost is rotted organic matter that gives nutrients to plants. Adding compost to soil makes it more fertile. Most things that come from plants can be turned into rich valuable compost. Animal droppings from pets—but not from cats or dogs—can also be used. The rotted compost can then be used on potted plants in your classroom.

Join three clear plastic bottles as shown in the picture. Use tape to attach the bottles. Make holes in the bottles to let in the air. Fill the column with vegetable peelings, grass cuttings, and other organic waste. Build two columns. Keep one wet and one dry to see which is the best way to make compost.

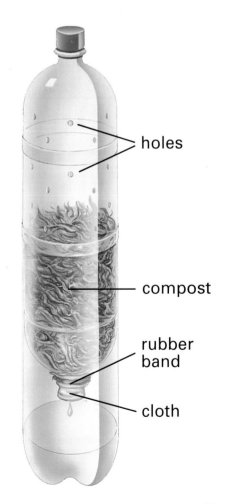

holes

compost

rubber band

cloth

Glossary

Agriculture   Another word for farming.

Biodiversity   The variety of living things.

Biotechnology   Science using plants and animals to create products for farming and industry.

Commercial   Doing something to make money.

Conserve   Keep from harm or loss.

Crop rotation   Growing different crops each year in the same field.

Developing countries   Poor countries that are developing better conditions for their people.

Digest   Break down and absorb food inside the body of an animal or a person.

Disease   Illness or sickness.

Erosion   Wearing away of the earth's surface.

Fertilizer   A substance that makes soil more fertile or productive.

Harvest   Gathering of grain or other crops.

Herbicide   A chemical that kills particular kinds of plants.

Intensive   Producing a lot from a small area.

Manure   Waste from animals.

Microscopic   Something so small that it cannot be seen without a microscope.

Nutrients   Things that feed plants and animals, including people.

Organic   Something that comes from plants or animals; not man-made.

Pesticides   Chemicals that kill pests, usually insects.

Population   Total number of people living in a town or a country.

Subsistence farming   When all the produce is eaten or used by the farmer and his family, with nothing left to sell.

Tropical   Countries or areas found between the Tropic of Cancer and the Tropic of Capricorn. Tropical countries have a warm climate.

Weed   Wild plant growing where it is not wanted.

Welfare   A good state of health and happiness.

Further Information

Books to Read

Anderson, Joan. *The American Family Farm: A Photo Essay*. San Diego: Harcourt Brace, 1996.

Bramwell, Martin, editor. *World Farming* (Usborne Understanding Geography). Tulsa, OK: EDC Publishing, 1994.

Cayne, Bernard S. and Jenny E. Tesar. *Food and Water: Threats, Shortages and Solutions* (Our Fragile Planet). New York: Facts on File, 1992.

Goldberg, Jake. *The Disappearing American Farm* (Impact Books—Issues). Danbury, CT: Franklin Watts, 1996.

Kerrod, Robin. *The World's Food Resources* (World's Resources). Austin, TX: Thomson Learning, 1993.

Morris, Scott E., editor. *Agriculture and Vegetation of the World* (Using and Understanding Maps). New York: Chelsea House, 1993.

Williams, Brian. *Farming*. Austin, TX: Raintree Steck-Vaughn, 1993.

Internet Sites

The BeWise Ranch website can be found at http://www.bewiseranch.com/contact/contact.htm

Index

32